⬐A STEP INTO HISTORY™⬏

THE VIETNAM WAR

BY STEVEN OTFINOSKI

Series Editor
Elliott Rebhun, Editor & Publisher,
The New York Times Upfront
at Scholastic

Content Consultant: James Marten, PhD, Professor and Chair, History
Department, Marquette University, Milwaukee, Wisconsin

Cover: U.S. soldiers disembark from a helicopter during the Vietnam War.

Library of Congress Cataloging-in-Publication Data
Names: Otfinoski, Steven, author.
Title: The Vietnam War / by Steven Otfinoski.
Description: New York, NY : Children's Press, an imprint of Scholastic Inc.,
    2017. | Series: A step into history | "Published simultaneously in
    Canada"—Title page verso. | Includes bibliographical references and index.
Identifiers: LCCN 2016043404| ISBN 9780531225707 (library binding) | ISBN
    9780531243640 (paperback)
Subjects: LCSH: Vietnam War, 1961–1975—Juvenile literature. | Vietnam War,
    1961-1975—Influence—Juvenile literature.
Classification: LCC DS557.7 .O84 2017 | DDC 959.704/3—dc23
LC record available at https://lccn.loc.gov/2016043404

All rights reserved. Published in 2017 by Children's Press, an imprint of
Scholastic Inc. Published simultaneously in Canada. Printed in Malaysia 108

SCHOLASTIC, CHILDREN'S PRESS, and associated logos are trademarks and/
or registered trademarks of Scholastic Inc.

1 2 3 4 5 6 7 8 9 10 R 26 25 24 23 22 21 20 19 18 17

CONTENTS

PROLOGUE

An American helmet and radio from the Vietnam War era

You will find the definitions of bold words in the glossary on pages 140–41.

AFTER WORLD WAR II, **COMMUNISM** SPREAD across Europe and Asia. The Soviet Union, China, North Korea, and North Vietnam were the world's key communist countries. Many Americans feared that communism would spread to the United States and drastically change the nation's way of life. The fear of communism also fueled the Cold War between the United States and the Soviet Union. They were locked in an intense economic, political, military, and ideological rivalry. It was called "cold" because the United States and the Soviet Union never directly fought each other. But the two countries were on opposite sides in many conflicts. The Vietnam War was one of them.

While war was raging in Vietnam, great social changes were taking place in the United States. The youth counterculture was questioning traditional values, and African Americans and women were protesting for civil rights. The same dissatisfaction that motivated these movements led to growing protests against the Vietnam War, taking place half a world away. As the conflict dragged on, it became one of the most unpopular and controversial wars in American history.

THE TWO SIDES
IN THE VIETNAM WAR

THE UNITED STATES OF AMERICA
and
SOUTH VIETNAM
(THE REPUBLIC OF VIETNAM)

South Vietnamese soldier

American soldier

NORTH VIETNAM
(THE DEMOCRATIC REPUBLIC OF VIETNAM)
and
THE VIET CONG
*Supported by the People's Republic
of China and the Soviet Union*

*North
Vietnamese
soldier*

*Viet Cong
guerrilla*

A guerrilla is a
member of a small
group of fighters or
soldiers that often
launches surprise
attacks against
official militaries.

MAPS

1954: FRENCH INDOCHINA

On the eve of the Vietnam War, the French colonies of Indochina included Laos, Cambodia, and Vietnam. Hanoi, in the far north of Vietnam, was the capital of French Indochina.

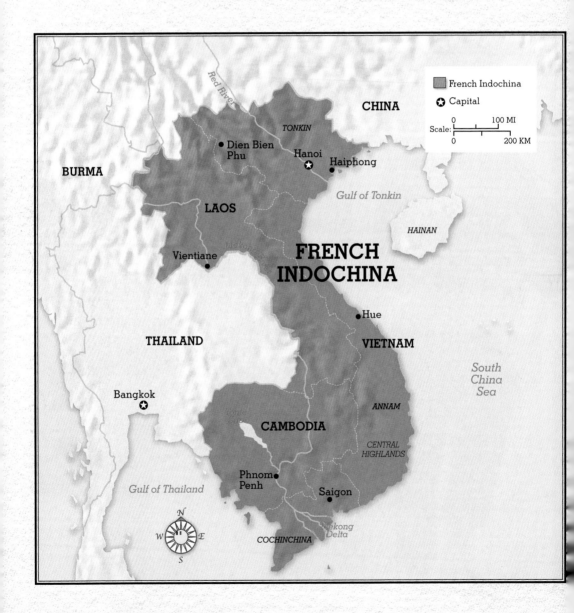

1954–75: NORTH VIETNAM AND SOUTH VIETNAM DURING THE WAR

Communist North Vietnam was supported by
Communist China to the north. South Vietnam
and Thailand were allies of the United States, but
Cambodia, Burma, and Laos remained neutral.

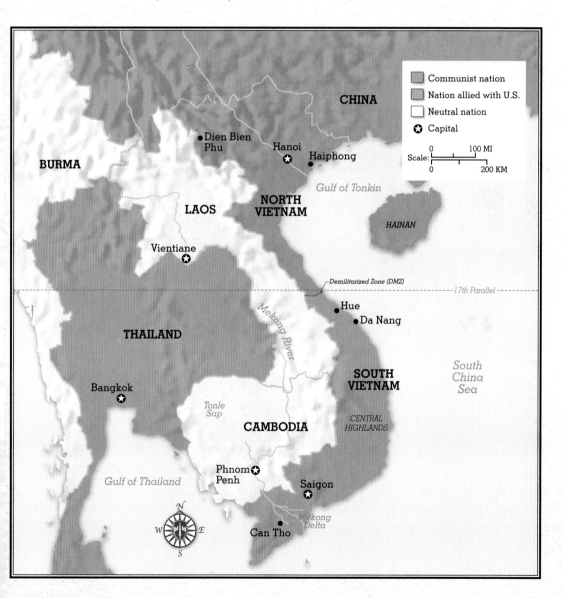

French colonists in Vietnam enjoy lunch sometime in the early 1900s.

CHAPTER 1

A LONG LEGACY

Vietnam struggled for independence and unity
for 2,000 years before the Vietnam War.

THROUGHOUT MUCH OF ITS HISTORY, VIETNAM has struggled for its freedom. Located in Southeast Asia, Nam Viet, as it was then called, was established as an independent kingdom in 200 BCE. Less than 100 years later, it was conquered by China.

Vietnam remained under Chinese control for the next thousand years. It gained its independence in 939 CE and remained independent until it was invaded by France in 1858.

Within 25 years, France made Vietnam part of its colonial empire, called French Indochina, which also included Laos and Cambodia. During World War II (1939–45), France was occupied by Germany. Japan, an ally of Germany, occupied French Indochina. Once again, Vietnam was a conquered country.

Japanese troops enter Saigon, Vietnam, on September 15, 1941, during World War II.

The flag of the Communist Party of Vietnam

CHAPTER 2

HO CHI MINH

North Vietnam's communist leader was
widely admired in his home country.

Find out more about people whose names appear in orange and bold on pages 134-35.

ONE OF THE KEY LEADERS IN VIETNAM'S struggle against the Japanese and the French was <u>Ho Chi Minh</u>. He was born in central Vietnam in 1890. At age 21, he left home to work as a cook on a French steamship. He spent several years traveling the world and then lived in England and later France, where he helped found the French Communist Party in 1920. Communists, including those who had come to power in Russia in 1917 and renamed it the Soviet Union, believed in a society where land, factories, and other resources were not owned by individuals, but controlled by the government.

Ho Chi Minh returned to Vietnam, where he formed the Indochina Communist Party in 1930. He believed communism offered the people of Vietnam the best way to improve their lives. Ho spent much of the next decade in exile, mostly in the Soviet Union. He finally returned home in 1940 to form an army called the Viet Minh and began fighting the Japanese, who had occupied the country earlier that year. When World War II ended with Japan's defeat in 1945, Viet Minh troops occupied the city of Hanoi in northern Vietnam. Ho proclaimed the North the independent Democratic Republic of Vietnam, a communist state.

Students carry a portrait of Ho Chi Minh during a parade through the streets of Hanoi, North Vietnam, in 1965.

French paratroopers drop
toward Dien Bien Phu in 1954.

CHAPTER 3

THE FRENCH RETURN

After World War II, the French returned to
reclaim their colonies in Southeast Asia, but
the Vietnamese wanted independence.

WITH THE DEFEAT OF JAPAN AND Germany in World War II, France returned to Indochina. However, it met resistance from Ho Chi Minh and the Viet Minh, who controlled most of Vietnam at the time. Fighting broke out between the French and the communist Viet Minh in December 1946. This conflict was called the Indochina War. U.S. **president Harry Truman** feared that if the Viet Minh won, all of Southeast Asia would fall to communism, an idea known as the domino theory.

Many Americans believed that communism threatened their democratic way of life. They had seen Eastern Europe fall under Soviet domination after World War II, beginning the Cold War between the United States and the Soviet Union that lasted for more than 40 years. Truman sent aid to France in the Indochina War. But despite having superior weapons and more troops, the French could not defeat the Viet Minh. Ho's soldiers used **guerrilla** tactics, striking unexpectedly in small bands and avoiding traditional battles. In 1954, the French set up a base of operations at the fortress of Dien Bien Phu in northwestern Vietnam.

A French officer uses a radio strapped to the back of a Vietnamese soldier in South Vietnam in 1951.

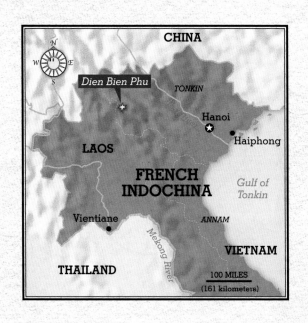

CHAPTER 4

AN UNEASY PEACE

As one war ended, another was just beginning.

THE BATTLE THAT FINALLY FORCED THE French out of Indochina was the Battle of Dien Bien Phu. The fort fell on May 7, 1954, with 12,000 French soldiers captured. Humiliated, the French abandoned Indochina. A peace settlement was drawn up in Geneva, Switzerland, in July 1954. Nine nations, including the United States, took part in the discussions. The Geneva **Accords** recognized communist North Vietnam and noncommunist South Vietnam as two temporarily separate zones. General elections were set to take place in both zones.

The elections were supposed to result in the unification of all Vietnam under a single president. Instead, both the North and the South declared themselves to be separate, independent nations. Ho Chi Minh strengthened his communist government in the North. South Vietnam elected Ngo Dinh Diem as its leader. Diem established a **republic** where the government was run by the people's elected representatives. But in practice, his government was increasingly **authoritarian**. Nonetheless, the United States preferred him to the communists and supported him with money and military guidance.

Near Hanoi, a French officer reads a newspaper announcing the end of the war in Indochina.

U.S. president Dwight Eisenhower greets South Vietnamese president Ngo Dinh Diem in Washington, D.C., in 1957.

CHAPTER 5

THE VIETNAM WAR BEGINS

The governments of the North and the South both felt that complete control of Vietnam was worth going to war over.

TENSIONS BETWEEN THE NORTH AND THE South grew. Diem was strongly opposed to communism. He also accused Ho of violating an agreement he made after the Indochina War to withdraw all Viet Minh guerrillas from the south. Soon after the Geneva Accords, communist guerrillas living in South Vietnam were assassinating village officials and terrorizing people.

Diem asked for increased U.S. aid to help defend his country. U.S. **president Dwight Eisenhower** thought that Ho had violated the Geneva Accords by secretly sending troops and supplies from the North to the South. Eisenhower sent American soldiers to South Vietnam as military advisers to help train its troops. But Diem's armed forces were poorly organized and corrupt. The U.S. advisers were unable to build an effective South Vietnamese army. The North Vietnamese were determined to win by conquest what they thought was rightfully theirs. They sent more guerrilla forces to South Vietnam to help those who had remained in the South. The Vietnam War had begun.

In Vietnam, it is called the American War. It is also sometimes called the Second Indochina War.

Not all historians agree about when the Vietnam War truly began. Many place the start date in 1954, while others believe the war began in 1955 or 1957.

An American military adviser plays with local children in a Vietnamese village in 1964.

*A Buddhist monk douses another
with gasoline during a protest in
Saigon, South Vietnam, in 1963.*

CHAPTER 6

THE FALL OF DIEM

Diem's corrupt government was overthrown,
not by the communists but by the
South Vietnamese military.

DIEM'S AUTHORITARIAN RULE WAS BECOMING increasingly unpopular. He forcibly moved villagers to new homes to keep the Viet Minh from influencing them. He also **censored** the press. A Roman Catholic, Diem discriminated against Buddhists, who rose in protest. Some Buddhists even set themselves on fire in the streets of Saigon in protests against Diem.

In January 1961, John F. Kennedy became the new U.S. president. Kennedy believed strongly in fighting communism. By mid-1962, he had sent thousands of additional U.S. troops to support Diem. Though still called "military advisers," these soldiers now took part in direct combat against the North Vietnamese.

Kennedy realized that Diem had lost the support of his people and tried to convince him to change, but it was too late. On November 1, 1963, South Vietnamese military leaders staged a **coup**. Diem was killed. The military **junta** that took over the government lasted only three months. General Nguyen Khanh emerged as the government's new leader. The United States continued to support him as it had Diem.

General Nguyen Khanh visits a South Vietnamese village along with U.S. secretary of defense Robert McNamara in 1964.

CHAPTER 7

THE GULF OF TONKIN RESOLUTION

President Lyndon Johnson asked Congress for authority to expand the U.S. role in Vietnam.

JUST THREE WEEKS AFTER THE DEATH OF Diem, President John F. Kennedy was assassinated in Dallas, Texas. Vice President **Lyndon Johnson** became president. Johnson assured the country that he would continue Kennedy's policies. One of those policies was to prevent the communists from taking over South Vietnam.

On August 5, 1964, Johnson reported to Congress and the nation that North Vietnamese planes had attacked two U.S. ships in the Gulf of Tonkin in South Vietnam. The president asked Congress for a **resolution** granting him the power to retaliate if necessary. All but two members of Congress voted to pass the Gulf of Tonkin Resolution. President Johnson now had the power to fight as he pleased in Vietnam without officially declaring war.

Secretary of Defense Robert McNamara explains the situation in the Gulf of Tonkin to the press in August 1964.

In 1967, a man emerges from a shelter in Hanoi, North Vietnam, to see if the sky is clear of U.S. bomber planes.

CHAPTER 8

OPERATION ROLLING THUNDER

The North Vietnamese were winning
the war, but President Johnson
was determined to stop them.

GENERAL KHANH'S CONTROL OVER SOUTH Vietnam did not last long. After he was ousted in another coup, a number of replacement governments came and went in quick succession. A weakened, politically unstable South Vietnam was coming dangerously close to losing the war. By April 1964, nearly two-thirds of the country's villages were controlled by the enemy.

President Johnson firmly believed in the domino theory and was determined to save South Vietnam from communism. In February 1965, he initiated Operation Rolling Thunder, an open-ended air bombing campaign against North Vietnam. On March 8, he sent 3,500 U.S. Marines ashore at the military base of Da Nang in South Vietnam. Although there were already 21,000 so-called military advisers in the country, these were the first official U.S. combat troops to arrive in Vietnam. As northern troops continued to invade South Vietnam, more American soldiers were deployed. By the end of 1965, there were 184,000 U.S. soldiers in South Vietnam.

It lasted for more than three years.

South Vietnamese soldiers parachute into the North in 1963.

*One of several flags used by
the Viet Cong during the war*

CHAPTER 9

THE VIET CONG

The Viet Cong were skilled, smart fighters who believed strongly in communism. This made them extremely effective military units.

"Viet Cong" is a shortened form of Viet Name Cong San, or "Vietnamese Communists."

I N ADDITION TO THE NORTH VIETNAMESE ARMY, the United States had to fight a powerful guerrilla force known as the Viet Cong. Formed in the mid-1950s, this organization was made up of both North and South Vietnamese people. Its fighters wanted to push the United States out of Vietnam and unify the country under communism. They had no headquarters, received their orders by word of mouth, were constantly on the move, and wore no uniforms. They blended in with the South Vietnamese population, which confused and frustrated U.S. troops. The American soldiers had a hard time telling **civilians** from enemies and whether or not they were in danger.

The Viet Cong struck with lightning speed when the United States least expected it. They were experts at ambushes, quick raids, and the planting of deadly mines and traps. Perhaps most important of all, the Viet Cong just seemed to keep on fighting no matter how many of them died in battle. This led many American soldiers to develop a reluctant respect for "Charlie," as they called the Viet Cong, while hating and fearing them at the same time.

Viet Cong soldiers travel through a swamp on their way to attack U.S. forces in South Vietnam in 1966.

An antiwar protest pin produced by a student group in 1970

CHAPTER 10

HAWKS AND DOVES

Back at home, a second war was developing
between Americans who supported
the war and those who did not.

BY 1966, THE ESCALATING WAR IN VIETNAM had divided Americans into two groups— hawks, who supported the war, and doves, who opposed it. Hawks sincerely believed that communism would quickly spread through all of Southeast Asia if South Vietnam fell. They urged President Johnson to wage war more aggressively and bring about a swift victory.

Doves thought the conflict in Vietnam was a civil war that the United States had no business being involved in. They saw American lives and millions of dollars being wasted in the war. They wanted the bombing to stop and the United States to negotiate a peace with the North Vietnamese.

Many young people were opposed to the war because they were the ones being called on to fight. College campuses became a focus of the antiwar movement. Students staged **sit-ins**, marches, and demonstrations. Some even broke the law by taking over college buildings and destroying property to make their point.

Former U.S. president Thomas Jefferson first used the term "war hawks" in a letter in 1798 to describe Americans who wanted to go to war with France.

College students in Boston, Massachusetts, march to protest the war in 1965.

"*Hell no, we won't go!***"**

—SLOGAN SHOUTED BY ANTIWAR
YOUTH WHO HAD BEEN DRAFTED

CHAPTER 11

THE DRAFT

The draft forced many young men into the war, while others fled the country.

ONE OF THE MAIN EVENTS OF MANY antiwar protests was the burning of **draft** cards by young men. By 1964, the Selective Service System (SSS), an agency overseeing military enlistment, began requiring American males from ages 18 to 25 to sign up for the draft. There weren't enough volunteers to fight in the war, so the draft was set up to force more people to join the military. Many Americans believed the draft was unjust. College students, many from middle-class families, could receive a draft **deferment**. This allowed them to stay in school instead of going to war. Young men who weren't in college were much more likely to be drafted.

About 100,000 Americans who were drafted avoided combat by <u>fleeing the country</u> during the war. These people were called draft dodgers. Some 90 percent of them went to Canada, where they were given legal immigrant status.

On January 21, 1977, his first day in office, President Jimmy Carter granted unconditional pardons to Vietnam draft evaders, allowing them to come home without facing criminal charges.

A protestor burns his draft card at a demonstration during the war.

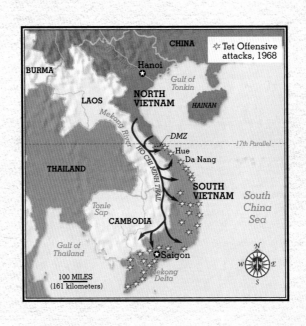

CHINA

BURMA

Hanoi ✪

☆ Tet Offensive
attacks, 1968

Gulf of
Tonkin

LAOS

NORTH
VIETNAM

HAINAN

Mekong River

DMZ

17th Parallel

Hue

Da Nang

THAILAND

HO CHI MINH TRAIL

SOUTH
VIETNAM

South
China
Sea

Tonle
Sap

CAMBODIA

Gulf of
Thailand

✪Saigon

Mekong
Delta

N

W   E

S

100 MILES
(161 kilometers)

CHAPTER 12

THE TET OFFENSIVE

An all-out assault from the North Vietnamese
and the Viet Cong failed to win the war, but its
psychological effects on Americans were devastating.

ON JANUARY 30, 1968, THE FIRST DAY OF TET, the Buddhist New Year in Vietnam, the North Vietnamese military and the Viet Cong launched a massive attack against South Vietnamese cities and towns. It took everyone by surprise. U.S. forces rushed to the defense of the cities and towns, leaving the countryside undefended. Even parts of Saigon, the capital, were seized by the enemy for a time.

After six weeks of heavy fighting, the communists retreated, exhausted by their efforts. They had failed in their attempt to take South Vietnam and had lost many men in the fighting. However, the American public was stunned and demoralized by the Tet Offensive. After all the promises from their leaders that the war would soon be over, it seemed that victory was farther away than ever. The antiwar movement grew stronger, and even staunch supporters of President Johnson in Congress were beginning to have their doubts that the war was winnable.

A South Vietnamese soldier runs for cover in Saigon during the Tet Offensive in 1968.

" *With each escalation, the world comes closer to the brink of cosmic disaster.* **"**

—CBS ANCHOR WALTER CRONKITE,
FEBRUARY 27, 1968

CHAPTER 13

THE LIVING ROOM WAR

It was the first war that the American
people could watch on television.

B Y 1965, MANY AMERICANS WERE BEGINNING to change their opinions about the war. Television reporters were right there in the villages and battlefields showing the American public just how chaotic and terrible war was. People were shocked by some of the things they saw on the evening news as they sat in their living rooms. They saw U.S. Marines destroy villages looking for Viet Cong. They saw the violent aftermath of attacks from the North Vietnamese. Even Walter Cronkite, the leading network news anchor and one of the most trusted men in America, was beginning to have his doubts about the war.

On February 27, 1968, Cronkite hosted a half-hour news special on CBS about the Tet Offensive, which he had witnessed firsthand on a trip to Vietnam. He ended the broadcast by predicting that the war would end in a bloody **stalemate** and that the only way out for the United States was to negotiate a peace. After watching the broadcast, President Johnson is said to have sadly told an aide, "If I've lost Cronkite, I've lost Middle America."

A woman in the United States watches footage of the war in her living room.

66 *I shall not seek, and I will not accept, the nomination of my party for another term as your president.* 99

—President Johnson in a national
broadcast on March 31, 1968

CHAPTER 14

JOHNSON DROPS A BOMBSHELL

The war had divided the country, and now it was about to bring down a president.

A MONTH AFTER CRONKITE'S BROADCAST, President Johnson went on television to address the American people. He announced that the United States would end all bombing in North Vietnam above the 20th **parallel** in hopes of encouraging leaders of the North Vietnamese government to participate in peace talks in Paris, France. Then he ended the speech by stating that he would not run for reelection that fall.

The announcement came as a complete surprise. Johnson hadn't even told members of his family about his decision not to run. Largely because the war was going so poorly, Johnson's popularity was at an all-time low, and he realized his chances of being reelected were slim. The peace talks began on May 13 but were hopelessly stalemated as the participants argued about how to organize the meeting. To further encourage the North Vietnamese to agree to peace, Johnson ordered all bombing of North Vietnam to end on October 31, 1968. However, the peace talks still failed to produce results.

President Johnson announces that he would not seek reelection in a televised address from the White House on March 31, 1968.

John Lennon (right) of the Beatles and his wife, artist Yoko Ono (left), hold up a poster protesting the war in London in 1969.

CHAPTER 15

SONGS OF PROTEST, SONGS OF WAR

The antiwar movement was fueled in part
by rock music and songs of protest.

IN POPULAR CULTURE, THE WAR WAS STRANGELY absent from film and television, outside of news programs. But it was very much alive in the music of America's youth counterculture. Pop songwriters wrote powerful songs against the war. They ranged from the dark humor of Country Joe and the Fish's "I-Feel-Like-I'm-Fixin'-to-Die Rag" to the more somber "For What It's Worth" by Buffalo Springfield. Canadian folk singer Buffy Sainte-Marie linked Vietnam to all the previous wars fought by humankind in her "Universal Soldier." In 1971, John Lennon and his wife, Yoko Ono, released the song "Happy Xmas (War Is Over)," which became an anthem for peace activists.

Antiwar feelings were also common in the era's soul music. Edwin Starr's "War" became a number-one hit in 1970. Marvin Gaye's "What's Going On" was partially inspired by the experiences of Gaye's brother as a soldier in Vietnam.

People who supported the war wrote songs, too. Staff Sergeant Barry Sadler's anthem to the special forces in Vietnam, "Ballad of the Green Berets," reached number one on the charts in 1966.

Folk singer Joan Baez performs at a demonstration against the war in London in May 1965.

AUGUST 26–29

The Democratic National Convention in Chicago is disrupted by internal fighting and clashes in the streets between antiwar demonstrators and police.

1968 JAN FEB MAR APR MAY JUN JUL AUG SEP

CHAPTER 16

THE ELECTION OF 1968

The war in Vietnam made the 1968 election one of the most tumultuous in American history.

Police made 589 arrests, and 119 police officers and 100 protesters were injured.

ON AUGUST 26, 1968, DEMOCRATS CONVERGED on Chicago for their national convention to pick a presidential candidate. Vice President Hubert Humphrey was the leading candidate. Humphrey said he wanted to negotiate a peace in Vietnam but felt that as vice president he had to defend the Johnson administration's policies. Democrats who wanted a promise of peace in the party's platform protested in the convention center. Outside, hundreds of <u>antiwar protesters clashed</u> with police, army troops, and National Guardsmen.

It was the most chaotic presidential convention in modern American history. Humphrey emerged as the candidate, but his connection to the Johnson administration made him unpopular with many voters. In November, he lost to Republican **Richard Nixon**, who won by 1 percent of the total votes cast. During the campaign, Nixon claimed he had a "secret plan" to end the war. The nation waited with anticipation to see what his plan was.

Delegates hold up signs protesting the war during the 1968 Democratic National Convention in Chicago.

President Richard Nixon delivers a speech on the Vietnam War on November 3, 1969.

CHAPTER 17

NIXON AND VIETNAMIZATION

President Nixon wanted to shift the burden of war from the United States to South Vietnam.

THE AMERICAN PEOPLE SAW LITTLE CHANGE in the government's war policies after Richard Nixon became president in January 1969, and no sign of a plan to end the war. Then, in November, Nixon told the nation during a televised address that he would begin withdrawing troops from Vietnam and shifting the burden of fighting the war to the South Vietnamese. Along with the ongoing peace talks, this "Vietnamization" of the war would, in Nixon's words, lead to "peace with honor."

By year's end, the number of U.S. troops in Vietnam was reduced from 540,000 to 479,000. A year later, it was down to 339,000. But little progress was made in the peace talks in Paris, and the war continued with increased bombing of North Vietnam. From the start of Nixon's presidency to March 1971, American planes dropped 2.5 million tons of bombs on Vietnam. That was more than America dropped on its enemies during all of World War II. For many Americans, pained by U.S. soldiers dying in a distant land, "peace with honor" still seemed a long way off.

About a third of all Americans who died in combat during the war were killed during Nixon's presidency.

U.S. Marines care for a wounded soldier in A Shau Valley, South Vietnam, in 1969.

A New York Daily News headline announces the expansion of the war into Cambodia on May 1, 1970.

CHAPTER 18

THE WAR WIDENS

While withdrawing troops from Vietnam,
Nixon sent other troops into Cambodia.

The Khmer Rouge eventually won the civil war and took control of Cambodia in 1975, killing more than one million people in the process.

SINCE 1963, THE NEIGHBORING COUNTRY OF Cambodia had reluctantly allowed North Vietnamese troops to conduct raids on South Vietnam from the eastern part of its territory. If Cambodia had refused, it would have risked being attacked itself. By 1970, the Viet Cong were thoroughly entrenched in eastern Cambodia. The Viet Cong also gave arms and money to the Khmer Rouge, communist **insurgents** led by Pol Pot in Cambodia.

President Nixon saw the Viet Cong presence in Cambodia as a threat. On April 30, 1970, he began sending U.S. and South Vietnamese troops into Cambodia to root out the Viet Cong and their supply centers. At the same time, a five-year civil war began between the U.S.-backed Cambodian government and the communist Khmer Rouge. Some Americans saw Nixon's expansion of the war into Cambodia and later neighboring Laos, which also harbored North Vietnamese troops, as a betrayal of his promise to end the war. A new wave of protests and demonstrations swept U.S. college campuses.

Check it out!

LAOS   NORTH VIETNAM

THAILAND

SOUTH VIETNAM

CAMBODIA

A young Khmer Rouge soldier patrols the streets of Phnom Penh, Cambodia, in 1975.

MAY 4

*Four students are
killed by National
Guardsmen at an antiwar
demonstration at Kent
State University in Ohio.*

1970 JAN FEB MAR APR MAY JUN JUL AUG

CHAPTER 19

TRAGEDY AT KENT STATE

Kent State University in Ohio
became a symbol of the violence and
division the war was causing in America.

KENT STATE UNIVERSITY IN OHIO WAS ONE of hundreds of colleges where students protested the invasion of Cambodia. When someone, possibly protesters, set fire to an army recruiting building on May 2, 1970, Governor James Rhodes sent in 900 National Guardsmen to stop the violence. On May 4, Guardsmen shot tear gas canisters to disperse a crowd of angry protesters. Some protesters threw the canisters and rocks back at the Guardsmen. Twenty-nine of the Guardsmen panicked and opened fire for 13 seconds. When the smoke cleared, four students were dead and nine others were wounded.

The tragedy at Kent State sent shockwaves across the nation. The next day, student strikes and demonstrations over the shootings spread to 448 college campuses. Criminal charges were brought against the Guardsmen who had fired, but the charges were later dismissed for lack of evidence. The dark day was memorialized in "Ohio," a song by Neil Young, with its haunting refrain "four dead in Ohio." Nixon ended the Cambodia campaign six weeks later.

Two of the students killed had not been part of the protest.

National Guardsmen confront a crowd of protesting students at Kent State University in 1970.

CHAPTER 20

THE MY LAI MASSACRE

One of the worst incidents of the
Vietnam War brought the morality of
the entire conflict into question.

THE WHOLE WORLD KNEW OF THE SHOOTINGS at Kent State within hours. However, it took more than a year and a half before the terrible details of the My Lai massacre in Vietnam came to light. On March 16, 1968, just 12 days after the incident at Kent State, American infantrymen, hardened by witnessing the deaths of many of their comrades, entered the South Vietnamese village of My Lai, believing it to be a Viet Cong stronghold. Under orders from Lieutenant William Calley, members of his **platoon** killed 109 civilians, including many women, children, and babies. Similar **atrocities** had been committed by the Viet Cong as well, especially against South Vietnamese civilians. But Americans wanted to believe that American soldiers would not commit such acts.

News of the incident didn't surface in the media until November 1969. Fourteen soldiers were charged in the massacre, but only Calley was convicted. He was sentenced to life in prison but served only three and a half years under house arrest. Calley's defense was that he was being unjustly singled out and that his commanding officers should also share responsibility for the massacre.

U.S. soldiers drive away after burning a village believed to be a Viet Cong stronghold in 1967.

The July 1, 1971, edition of the New York Times *displays a front-page headline about the Pentagon Papers.*

CHAPTER 21

THE PENTAGON PAPERS

The Pentagon Papers showed that the U.S. government had not always been honest with the American people about the war in Vietnam.

A MONG THE FORMER SUPPORTERS OF THE WAR who had grown disillusioned was a military analyst named Daniel Ellsberg. Ellsberg had helped write a secret report on U.S. involvement in Vietnam ordered by the Department of Defense. However, he felt that the report hid the truth about government involvement and needed to be made public. Ellsberg photocopied part of the report and gave it to the *New York Times* and the *Washington Post*, two of the nation's most important newspapers. The *New York Times* published its first article with excerpts from the report on June 13, 1971. The Department of Justice got a federal court to temporarily halt further publication, but when the case came before the Supreme Court in late June, it ruled in favor of the newspapers.

The so-called Pentagon Papers showed the wide gap between what four presidential administrations had told the American people and what they were actually doing in secret. Among the many revelations was that the government knew about the coup to overthrow President Diem in 1963 and did nothing to stop it. The Pentagon Papers put more pressure on Nixon to bring the war to a swift end.

In June 2011, the 40th anniversary of the Pentagon Papers' first appearance, the National Archives released the complete reports, numbering 7,000 pages in 48 boxes.

Daniel Ellsberg (left) and his wife (right) celebrate outside a Los Angeles courthouse after the Pentagon Papers case against Ellsberg was dismissed by a judge in 1973.

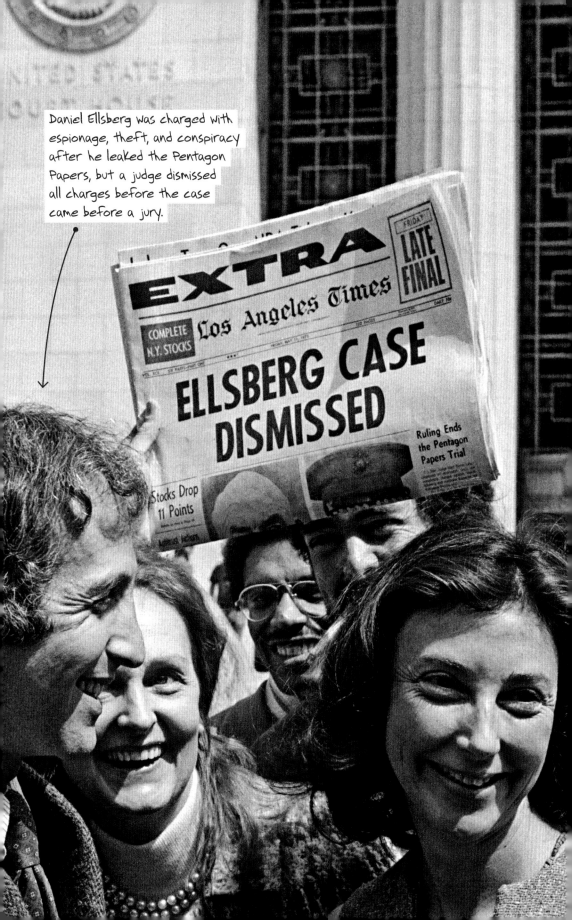

Daniel Ellsberg was charged with espionage, theft, and conspiracy after he leaked the Pentagon Papers, but a judge dismissed all charges before the case came before a jury.

*Children flee from their homes
after South Vietnamese planes
dropped a napalm bomb on a
village outside of Saigon.*

CHAPTER 22

NAPALM AND AGENT ORANGE

In Vietnam, chemical weapons proved to
be as deadly as more conventional weapons.

AMERICAN FORCES IN VIETNAM OFTEN used napalm, a jellied form of gasoline, in bombs and flame throwers. The jelly splattered on impact and clung to a victim's skin, causing horrible burns. Many Viet Cong and innocent civilians were killed or maimed by napalm.

Agent Orange was another dangerous chemical weapon used by U.S. forces. A cocktail of weed killers, this chemical was sprayed from American planes to **defoliate** trees and reveal Viet Cong hideouts. It also was used to destroy enemy crops.

By the early 1970s, it was discovered that Agent Orange contained dioxin, a chemical that causes cancer and birth defects. Many American Vietnam veterans developed symptoms years later that they believed were caused by exposure to Agent Orange. The veterans sued the companies that made the chemical, leading to years of lawsuits. Eventually the companies created a relief fund for these victims and their families.

U.S. planes drop Agent Orange near Saigon in 1970.

❝ *[H]ow do you ask a man to be the last man to die in Vietnam? How do you ask a man to be the last man to die for a mistake?* **❞**

—NAVAL LIEUTENANT JOHN KERRY
SPEAKING BEFORE THE SENATE FOREIGN
RELATIONS COMMITTEE IN APRIL 1971

CHAPTER 23

VETS AGAINST THE WAR

Some of the most vocal critics of the
war were men who fought in it.

VIETNAM VETERANS OFTEN CAME HOME to less than a hero's welcome. As the war became more unpopular, returning soldiers were ignored or forgotten by many Americans. Veterans, often just called "vets," had difficulty finding work in civilian life and often received poor medical care for their injuries at Veterans Administration hospitals. Some veterans felt their sacrifice had been made in a war that was unjust or shouldn't have been fought at all. In 1967, they banded together to form the Vietnam Veterans Against the War (VVAW).

In April 1971, more than 1,000 VVAW members met in Washington, D.C., and marched to the U.S. Capitol. Each one of them made a statement and then threw their war medals onto the steps of the Capitol.

John Kerry, a leader of the VVAW, later became a U.S. senator from Massachusetts and then served as secretary of state under President Barack Obama. "I saw courage both in the Vietnam War and in the struggle to stop it," Kerry has said. "I learned that patriotism includes protest, not just military service."

Members of the VVAW gather in Washington, D.C., to protest the war in December 1971.

*A mortar bomb from
the Vietnam War*

CHAPTER 24

TROUBLE IN THE CENTRAL HIGHLANDS

Just when it looked like hostilities were
ending, the war heated up again.

B Y THE END OF 1971, ONLY 156,800 U.S. GROUND troops remained in Vietnam, and their numbers were dropping rapidly. Nixon was making good on his commitment to "Vietnamize" the war. Then, on March 30, 1972, the North Vietnamese launched a major offensive in South Vietnam's Central Highlands. Nixon responded by ordering renewed bombing of the North. He also commanded navy aircraft to plant mines in Haiphong, North Vietnam's main harbor, to stop supply ships from coming in. The invasion of the Central Highlands was halted soon afterward.

The Viet Cong suffered many casualties, but they occupied large sections of South Vietnam and were far from beaten. The South Vietnamese had survived the assault but were exhausted. The American troops still remaining in the country as Nixon's Vietnamization continued were demoralized. Both sides were ready to try once again to negotiate a peace.

South Vietnamese soldiers keep watch from a bunker in Kontum City in the Central Highlands in 1972.

JANUARY 13

North Vietnam and the
United States sign a peace
treaty in Paris, France.

1973 JAN FEB MAR APR MAY JUN JUL AUG

CHAPTER 25

THE PARIS PEACE ACCORDS

Through tough negotiations, the United
States found a way out of the war.

THE PEACE TALKS THAT HAD BEGUN IN 1968 resumed in Paris with the approval of China and the Soviet Union, both supporters of North Vietnam. The U.S. negotiator in the Paris peace talks was **National Security Adviser Henry Kissinger**. North Vietnam was represented by a **diplomat** named **Le Duc Tho**. During the 1972 talks, Kissinger made big promises to the North Vietnamese. The United States would completely withdraw from Vietnam. In return, North Vietnam would release all U.S. prisoners of war. While the United States and North Vietnam agreed to these terms, South Vietnam was hesitant to sign the treaty. The fighting continued for several more months. Finally, South Vietnam gave in near the end of 1972. On January 13, 1973, the countries signed a final peace agreement.

Kissinger and Tho were jointly awarded the Nobel Peace Prize in 1973 for their efforts, but Tho declined to accept the award. He claimed that the United States had already violated points of the agreement by encouraging South Vietnam to keep fighting. Despite the peace agreement, fighting continued in Vietnam between the North and South for more than a year and a half.

Henry Kissinger (right) shakes hands with Le Duc Tho (left) in Paris, France, in 1973.

A Vietnamese man weeps as he walks along the "Convoy of Tears" in 1975.

CHAPTER 26

THE "CONVOY OF TEARS"

A treaty had been signed, but there was still
no peace for the people of South Vietnam.

WITH ALL U.S. TROOPS WITHDRAWN from the war by March 1973, the South Vietnamese were left to fight on their own. With increasing strength, the North Vietnamese and their Viet Cong allies took over the country, city by city and town by town. In March 1975, they launched a large-scale offensive in the Central Highlands, leading to the fall of the city of Ban Me Thout. The South Vietnamese forces retreated toward the south, followed by some 400,000 civilians, including soldiers' relatives, deserters, and minor government workers. They were attacked every step of the way by North Vietnamese artillery and by their own air force, who fired on them in the confusion. Almost all of the refugees died or were wounded along the way. Only a very few of them made it to safety farther south while traveling along what has come to be called the "**convoy** of tears."

On April 21, South Vietnamese president Nguyen Van Thieu delivered a three-hour farewell speech on South Vietnamese television. He denounced the United States for abandoning his country. Five days later, he left Saigon on a plane to Taiwan.

Refugees ride aboard a truck heading out of Saigon, South Vietnam, in 1975.

APRIL 30

*Saigon, the capital of
South Vietnam, falls to
the North Vietnamese;
the Vietnam War ends.*

1975 JAN FEB MAR APR MAY JUN JUL AUG

CHAPTER 27

THE FALL OF SAIGON

The final evacuation of the city was chaotic and cruel. Many South Vietnamese were left behind to face the North Vietnamese victors.

ON APRIL 30, 1975, NORTH VIETNAMESE TROOPS closed in on the South Vietnamese capital city of Saigon. U.S. Marines were prepared to evacuate Americans from the U.S. **Embassy** compound. To allow enough space for large helicopters to land, men cut down trees in the embassy garden. Seventy desperate people crammed into the first helicopter. It was supposed to hold only 50. The pilot of the heavily weighted copter managed to lift off into the sky with North Vietnamese bullets flying all around. The copter's passengers were among the lucky few who managed to escape. In one of the most dramatic moments of the war, hundreds of South Vietnamese clamored to get out in the other copters. They were desperate and terrified of what would happen to them with the North Vietnamese in control of the country. However, most were left behind.

Meanwhile, enemy tanks crashed through the gates of the building where General Duong Van Minh, the country's final president, awaited. Saigon had fallen, and with it went the rest of South Vietnam. The North Vietnamese would soon rename it Ho Chi Minh City after the communist leader who had died in 1969.

Thousands of South Vietnamese refugees were later admitted into the United States where they succeeded in starting new lives.

A CIA employee helps Vietnamese evacuees onto a helicopter near the U.S. Embassy in 1975.

A flag honoring American prisoners of war (POW) and missing-in-action (MIA) soldiers of the Vietnam War

CHAPTER 28

BITTER LESSONS

Spanning four presidencies, Vietnam was the
longest war the United States had ever fought.

A TOTAL OF 58,220 AMERICAN SOLDIERS died in the Vietnam War, and 304,000 others were wounded. As many as four million Vietnamese—both soldiers and civilians—died. The war cost the United States $168 billion in military expenses. It divided the nation and is still a controversial subject for many Americans today. It also eroded many Americans' trust in the actions of their government.

The war taught the people of the United States important lessons. The government and its leaders need to be honest with Congress and the American people about their goals and strategies before entering into any conflict. It is also important to have strong, clear reasons to go to war.

Americans also remembered, once more, that wars are extremely painful for both winners and losers.

American veterans who lost their legs in the war participate in a parade in New York City in 1973 to honor those who fought in the war.

College student Maya Lin won the competition to design the Vietnam Veterans Memorial in Washington, D.C.

CHAPTER 29

THE VIETNAM VETERANS MEMORIAL

Some people criticize it as a tombstone.

Others call it "the wall that heals."

The memorial was paid for with
$9 million in private contributions.

AFTER THE WAR, A GROUP OF VIETNAM vets formed an organization to <u>raise money</u> to build a memorial to those who died in the war. A nationwide competition for the memorial's design received more than 1,400 entries. The winning design, chosen in 1981, was by Maya Lin, a 21-year-old college student. The Vietnam Veterans Memorial, built in Washington, D.C., is a long wall of black polished granite engraved with the names of more than 58,000 Americans killed or reported missing in the war. The memorial was dedicated on November 13, 1982. Two years later, a sculpture of three Vietnam servicemen was added to the memorial.

The memorial receives more than three million visitors a year. Some visitors are family and friends of the dead. Others come to pay their respects to the soldiers who sacrificed their lives. Many people leave flowers, notes, artwork, and other remembrances at the memorial. The thousands of items left each year are collected and preserved by staff members. The memorial is a reminder of the sacrifice made in Vietnam and the terrible cost of war.

The Vietnam Veterans Memorial in Washington, D.C., helps people remember the thousands of Americans who died fighting in Vietnam.

*Today, Ho Chi Minh City is
a thriving center of activity.*

CHAPTER 30

A BOND OF FRIENDSHIP

Time has helped heal the wounds between the
United States and Vietnam in remarkable ways.

TODAY, MORE THAN 40 YEARS AFTER THE war's end, Vietnam is no longer an enemy but a friend of the United States. The two nations are trading partners that import and export millions of dollars worth of goods each year. Nearly 500,000 American tourists visit Vietnam each year, and nearly 19,000 Vietnamese students are studying in American universities. In 2016, Fulbright University Vietnam, an American school for Vietnamese, opened in Ho Chi Minh City. As of 2014, Vietnamese immigrants were the sixth-largest immigrant group in America, numbering 1.3 million.

In May 2016, President Barack Obama became the third consecutive U.S. president to visit Vietnam. While the two countries still have their differences, they have found much common ground. "It has taken many years and required great effort," Obama said in a speech while in Vietnam. "But now we can say something that was once unimaginable. Today, Vietnam and the United States are partners."

President Barack Obama (left) shakes hands with Vietnamese president Tran Dai Quang (right) in front of a bust of Ho Chi Minh in Hanoi in 2016.

President Harry Truman (1945–53) believed that if Vietnam fell to the communists, then all Southeast Asia would follow. This was known as the domino theory. As a result, his administration gave aid to the French in their fight to retake their colony of Vietnam from the communist Viet Minh in the Indochina War.

President Dwight Eisenhower (1953–61) sent U.S. military advisers to Vietnam after the French left and hostilities between the North and the South erupted into war in 1957.

President Lyndon Johnson (1963–69) entered office after the assassination of John F. Kennedy. He began to send U.S. troops to fight alongside the South Vietnamese in 1965. The war escalated and eventually became more unpopular with the American people. As a result, Johnson decided not to run for reelection in 1968.

President Richard Nixon (1969–74) succeeded Johnson in the White House after promising peace in Vietnam. He ended U.S. involvement in the war in 1973, withdrawing all U.S. troops.

National Security Adviser Henry Kissinger represented the United States in the Paris peace talks and negotiated the final peace treaty in January 1973. He was awarded, with Le Duc Tho, the Nobel Peace Prize in 1973.

Le Duc Tho represented North Vietnam in the Paris peace talks and was awarded, with Kissinger, the Nobel Peace Prize in 1973. He declined to accept the award, claiming that the United States had not been faithful to parts of the treaty.

President Ho Chi Minh of North Vietnam led the country's communist government from the 1940s until he died of a heart attack in 1969. Even after his death, he remained an important symbol of leadership for communist forces in Vietnam.

President Ngo Dinh Diem of South Vietnam was elected in 1955. Although his country was a republic, Diem ran it with an authoritarian hand, making him unpopular. He was overthrown and killed by the military in 1963, leading to a long string of ineffective governments in South Vietnam.

VIETNAM WAR TIMELINE

1955
The republic of South Vietnam is established by President Ngo Dinh Diem.

NOVEMBER 1
The Diem government is overthrown by South Vietnamese military leaders.

1946
The Indochina War between France and Vietnam begins.

1946 **1954** **1955** **1957** **1963** **1964**

1957
U.S. president Dwight Eisenhower sends military advisers to help the South Vietnamese in their fight against the North Vietnamese.

1954
France exits the Indochina War after its defeat at the Battle of Dien Bien Phu. The Vietnam War begins.

AUGUST 5
The U.S. Congress passes the Gulf of Tonkin Resolution, giving President Lyndon Johnson the power to wage undeclared war against North Vietnam.

FEBRUARY

*Johnson initiates
Operation Rolling
Thunder, an air bombing
campaign against
North Vietnam.*

JANUARY 30

*The North Vietnamese
launch the Tet Offensive,
a massive assault on
South Vietnam.*

MARCH 31

*President Johnson tells
the nation he will not run
for a second full term.*

1965 **1967** **1968** JAN FEB MAR APR MAY JUN JUL AUG SEP OCT NOV DEC

MARCH 8

*About 3,500 U.S. Marines
become the first U.S.
combat troops to arrive
in South Vietnam.*

FEBRUARY 27

*CBS news anchor Walter
Cronkite declares that
the war is unwinnable
on a national television
news special.*

AUGUST 26–29

*The Democratic National
Convention in Chicago
is disrupted by internal
fighting and clashes in the
streets between antiwar
demonstrators and police.*

JANUARY
Richard Nixon, who campaigned with a "secret plan" to end the war, becomes president.

DECEMBER
A draft lottery for eligible men ages 18 to 25 begins.

MAY 4
Four students are killed by National Guardsmen at an antiwar demonstration at Kent State University in Ohio.

JUNE 13
The New York Times *publishes the first excerpts from the Pentagon Papers.*

1969 JFMAMJJASOND **1970** JFMAMJJASOND **1971** JFMAMJJASOND **1972** JF

NOVEMBER
Nixon begins his plan of "Vietnamization," reducing American troops in Vietnam and putting more of the war in the hands of the South Vietnamese.

APRIL 30
Nixon sends American troops and bomber planes into Cambodia to destroy North Vietnamese hideouts and supply centers.

MARCH 30
The North Vietnamese launch a major assault on South Vietnam's Central Highlands.

APRIL
More than 1,000 members of Vietnam Veterans Against the War march in Washington, D.C.

JANUARY 13

North Vietnam and the United States sign a peace treaty in Paris, France.

MARCH

North Vietnam begins another major offensive on South Vietnam; close to 400,000 fleeing civilians are killed on the road south in what is called "the convoy of tears."

NOVEMBER 13

The Vietnam Veterans Memorial in Washington, D.C., is dedicated.

S O N D **1973** J F M A M J J A S O N D **1975** **1982** **2016**

MARCH

All U.S. troops are withdrawn from Vietnam.

APRIL 30

Saigon, the capital of South Vietnam, falls to the North Vietnamese; the Vietnam War ends.

MAY 23–25

President Barack Obama visits Vietnam to further ties between the two nations.

GLOSSARY

- **accords** (uh-KORDZ) signed agreements between countries about the way they will deal with something that concerns them

- **atrocities** (uh-TRAH-suh-teez) very cruel or terrible actions

- **authoritarian** (uh-thor-uh-TARE-ee-uhn) demanding total submission to a government

- **censored** (SEN-surd) removed parts of a book, movie, or other work that are thought to be unacceptable or offensive

- **civilians** (suh-VIL-yuhnz) people who are not members of the armed forces or a police force

- **communism** (KAHM-yoo-niz-uhm) a way of organizing the economy of a country so that all the land, property, businesses, and resources belong to the government or community instead of individuals

- **convoy** (KAHN-voi) a group of vehicles or ships that travel together for safety or convenience

- **coup** (KOO) the often violent overthrow of a government by a group within that country

- **deferment** (di-FUR-muhnt) postponement until later

- **defoliate** (dee-FOH-lee-ate) to strip trees of their leaves

- **diplomat** (DIP-luh-mat) someone who officially represents his or her country's government in a foreign country

- **draft** (DRAFT) a system that requires people to serve in the armed forces

- **embassy** (EM-buh-see) the official place in a foreign country where an ambassador and other diplomats work

- **guerrilla** (guh-RIL-uh) relating to a small group of fighters or soldiers who do not belong to a regular army and often launch surprise attacks against an official army, making it hard for their opponents to tell if they are civilians or soldiers

- **insurgents** (in-SUR-jintz) rebels fighting against an established government

- **junta** (HOON-tuh) a group of military officers that rules a country after seizing power

- **parallel** (PAR-uh-lel) any of the imaginary lines that circle the earth parallel to the equator

- **platoon** (pluh-TOON) a group of soldiers made up of two or more squads

- **republic** (ri-PUHB-lik) a form of government in which the people have the power to elect representatives who run the government

- **resolution** (rez-uh-LOO-shuhn) a formal decision voted for by Congress or another governing body

- **sit-ins** (SIT-inz) peaceful protests in which protesters occupy a public space and refuse to leave

- **stalemate** (STALE-mate) a situation that results in a deadlock, with no progress possible

FIND OUT MORE

BOOKS

Caputo, Philip. *10,000 Days of Thunder: A History of the Vietnam War*. New York: Atheneum Books for Young Readers, 2005.

Herr, Michael. *Dispatches*. New York: Vintage Books, 1991.

O'Brien, Tim. *The Things They Carried*. New York: Mariner Books, 2009.

Warren, Andrea. *Escape from Saigon: How a Vietnam War Orphan Became an American Boy*. New York: Square Fish, 2008.

FILMS

Full Metal Jacket (1987). DVD, Warner Home Video, 2007.

Good Morning, Vietnam (1987). DVD, Buena Vista Home Entertainment, 2006.

The Killing Fields (1984). DVD, Warner Home Video, 2001.

Platoon (1986). DVD, MGM, 2011.

NOTE: Some books and films may not be appropriate for younger viewers.

VISIT THIS SCHOLASTIC WEB SITE FOR MORE
INFORMATION ABOUT **THE VIETNAM WAR**
www.factsfornow.scholastic.com
Enter the keywords **THE VIETNAM WAR**

INDEX

Page numbers in *italics* indicate illustrations.

ABOUT THE AUTHOR

Steven Otfinoski has written more than 180 books for young readers. They include many books about wars and soldiers. Three of his books have been named to the New York Public Library's list of recommendations, Books for the Teen Age. He lives with his family in Connecticut.